D1452241

Des Knaben Wunderhorn
and the Rückert Lieder

for Voice and Piano

Gustav Mahler

English Translations by
Stanley Appelbaum • John Bernhoff • Addie Funk

DOVER PUBLICATIONS, INC.
Mineola, New York

Mahler's orchestral settings of three texts
from *Des Knaben Wunderhorn* are available
in the following Dover editions:

For "Urlicht"
Symphonies Nos. 1 and 2 in Full Score
(Dover 0-486-25473-9)

•

For "Es sungen drei Engel" and "Das himmlische Leben"
Symphonies Nos. 3 and 4 in Full Score
(Dover 0-486-25473-9)

Bibliographical Note

This Dover edition, first published in 1999, is a new compilation of the following Mahler
songs, originally published separately.
  B. Schott's Söhne, Mainz, originally published the following nine settings in the collection
14 Lieder und Gesänge (aus der Jugendzeit) . . . von Gustav Mahler, n.d.: "Ablösung im
Sommer" / "Aus! Aus!" / "Ich ging mit Lust . . ." / "Nicht wiedersehen!" / "Scheiden und
Meiden" / "Selbstgefühl" / "Starke Einbildungskraft" / "Um schlimme Kinder . . ." and
"Zu Strassburg . . ."
  Universal-Edition originally published the following twelve settings in the two-volume
collection *12 Gesänge aus "Des Knaben Wunderhorn"*: "Wer hat dies Liedlein erdacht?"
(1913; English version, 1920) / "Der Schildwache Nachtlied" and "Urlicht" (both, 1914)
/ "Verlorne Müh'" (1914; English version, 1920) / "Trost im Unglück" (English version,
1920) / "Das irdische Leben" (1920) / and five settings, n.d.: "Es sungen drei Engel . . .,"
"Lied des Verfolgten . . .," "Lob des hohen Verstands," "Rheinlegendchen" and "Wo die
schönen Trompeten blasen."
  C. F. Kahnt Nachfolger, Leipzig, originally published "Der Tamboursg'sell" and
"Revelge" (both, 1905) as well as the five Rückert songs—all 1905 except for "Liebst du um
Schönheit (1907)—in *Gustav Mahler, Sieben Lieder aus letzter Zeit.*
  The annotated composite contents list is newly added. Stanley Appelbaum graciously pro-
vided the glossary and English translations specially for this edition. His earlier translations
of "Das himmlische Leben" and "Urlicht" first appeared, respectively, in Dover's full-score
editions of Mahler's Symphony No. 4 and Symphony No. 2. English underlays by Addie
Funk and by John Bernhoff are reproduced as they appeared in their original publications.
  We are grateful to the Stanford University Music Library for providing the original edition
of Universal's *Mahler, 12 Gesänge*, Volume 2.

International Standard Book Number: 0-486-40634-2

Manufactured in the United States of America
Dover Publications, Inc., 31 East 2nd Street, Mineola, N.Y. 11501

CONTENTS

•

24 Songs to Texts from *Des Knaben Wunderhorn*
(The Boy's Miraculous Horn)
(1892–1901)
Arranged for voice and piano by the composer

*"Das himmlische Leben" was written in 1892 as part of Mahler's five *Humoresken*, but the composer's arrangement for voice and piano remained unpublished until 1993. While his music in this version is unavailable for the present edition, Mahler's orchestral setting of the text is published in Dover's full-score edition of Symphonies Nos. 3 and 4 *(see p. iv)*.

•

Five Rückert Songs
Songs to Poems by Friedrich Rückert
(1901–2)
Arranged for voice and piano by the composer

GLOSSARY

barsch, harshly
bitterlich, bitterly
breite Triolen, broad triplets
Büble, boy

das Mädchen, the girl
der Gefangene, the prisoner
drängend, with urgency
durchaus zart, extremely gently

ein wenig gemäßigter als im Anfang, a little more moderate
    than at the beginning
ein wenig zurückhaltend, holding back a little
etwas, somewhat, rather
    bewegter, with somewhat more motion
    langsamer, a bit slower
    zurückhaltend, holding back somewhat

Fistel, falsetto

gänzlich ersterbend, dying away altogether
gemächlich, at a comfortable tempo [*Comodo*]

immer (stark) mit Pedal, always with (a heavy use of) pedal
im Volkston (ohne Sentimentalität, äusserst rythmisch), in folk
    style (without sentimentality, extremely rhythmic)
in gemessenem Marschtempo, in moderate march tempo
in verdriesslichem Ton, in a peevish tone

keck, jauntily
keckes Marschtempo, jaunty march tempo
kläglich (mit Parodie), lamenting (as a parody)
kurzer Halt, brief pause

leidenschaftlich (eigenwillig) (aber zart), passionately
    (willfully) (but gently)
leise, zögernd, softly, hesitantly
linke Hand, left hand
lustig, merrily
lustig im Tempo und keck im Ausdruck, at a merry tempo,
    with a jaunty expression

Mädchen, girl
mit, with
    Aufschwung, with impetus
    Humor, humorously
    Pedal, with pedal
    starkem Pedalgebrauch, with a heavy use of the pedal
    steigerndem Ausdruck, with increasing expression
munter, brisk

nicht schleppen / Choralmäßig, don't drag / like a chorale

Oberstimme etwas hervortretend, the upper notes rather
    prominent
ohne Ped(al), without pedal

possierlich, in a droll manner

sanft, gently
Schalmei, shepherd's pipe
schaudernd, with a shudder
schnell steigernd, quickly accelerating
schwermüthig, melancholy
sehr, very
    feierlich, aber schlicht, very solemn, but simple
    gehalten, very steady
    gemächlich, mit humoristischem Ausdruck, at a very
        comfortable tempo, with humorous expression
    hervortretend, quite prominently
    leidenschaftlich, aber zart, very passionately, but gently
    zart, very gently
streng im Takt, strictly in measure

träumerisch, durchaus zart, dreamily, tenderly throughout

verärgert, disgruntled
verklingend, dying away
verträumt, dreamy
verzagt, schmeichlerisch, timidly, flatteringly

wieder langsam, wie zu Anfang, slow again, as at the beginning
wie eine Schalmei, like a shepherd's pipe

wie fernes Glockenläuten, like a distant tolling of bells
wie früher, as earlier [comparing note values]
wie (im) (zu) Anfang, as at the beginning
wie Trompetenmusik, like trumpet music
wie vorher, as before

zart, gently
zart hervortretend, slightly prominent
zurückhaltend (unmerklich), holding back (imperceptibly)

•

Footnotes and longer score notes

p. 2

*Von [bis] kann die Gesangsstimme eventuell nach
Bedürfniss des Sängers weggelassen werden.*
The bracketed vocal line can be omitted if the singer
needs to do so.

p. 45, 101

*Die kleinen Noten vom Sänger nur im Nothfalle zu
gebrauchen.*
The singer is to use the small notes only when this is
absolutely unavoidable.

p. 90

*Im Nothfalle kann vom Spieler das ganze Stück hin-
durch die obere Oktave in der linken Hand fortgelassen
werden.*
If absolutely necessary, the pianist may omit the upper
octave in the left hand throughout the piece.

p. 103

*Zur Erleichterung des Spielers kann in beiden Händen die
untere Oktave weggelassen werden.*
To simplify the execution, the lower octave in both
hands can be omitted.

p. 119

*Oberstimme der rechten Hand über die Gesangstimme
hervortretend*
The upper notes of the right hand prominent above the
vocal part

p. 124

*In allen diesen tiefen Trillern ist mit Hilfe des Pedals der
Klang gedämpfter Trommeln nachzuahmen.*
In all these low trills, the sound of muffled drums is to
be imitated with the help of the pedal.

p. 127

*Die unteren Noten für Sänger, die über keine Kopfstimme
verfügen.*
The notes printed lower are for singers who do not
possess head tones.

TEXT TRANSLATIONS
From *Des Knaben Wunderhorn* ("The Boy's Miraculous Horn")

Folksongs and folksong-style poems collected, retouched, or made up out of whole cloth by Achim von Arnim (1781–1831) and Clemens Brentano (1778–1842); published 1806 and 1808.

English translations given below are by Stanley Appelbaum. Words in parentheses are Mahler's additions to the text, but his numerous omissions and alterations are mostly incorporated without comment. Additional translations by Addie Funk or by John Bernhoff appear in the music as text underlays and are not reprinted here; they are indicated below by the writer's initials [A.F.] or [J.B.] under the title.

Ablösung im Sommer
Changing of the guard in summertime

The cuckoo has taken a fatal fancy
To a green willow! (Cuckoo is dead! He took a fatal fancy!)
Who, then, is to help us pass the time
And chase away boredom all summer long?
Ho! Lady Nightingale shall do that!
She sits on a green branch!
(The fine little nightingale, the dear, sweet nightingale!)
She sings and jumps, and is always merry
When other birds are silent!
We're waiting for Lady Nightingale,
Who lives in the green hedgerow,
And when the cuckoo is finished,
She begins to sing!

Aus! Aus!
Out! Out! (Over! Over!)

"Today we are marching, (Hurray, in the green Maytime)
Tomorrow we are marching
Out through the high town gate!"

"Are you leaving already? (Oh, oh, my darling!)
Are you never coming back home?" [REPEATS]

"Ah, you dark-haired girl,
Our love is not yet over!

"Drink a glass of wine
To your health and mine!
Do you see this plume on my hat?
Now it's time to march as if we meant it!
Take the handkerchief out of my pocket,
Dry away your tears with it!

"Today we are marching . . . " *(etc.)*

"I shall enter a convent
Because my sweetheart is leaving!
Where are you off to, darling?
Are you leaving as early as today?
And never coming back?
Ah, how gloomy it will be
Here in town!
How soon will you forget me,
Poor girl that I am?"

"Tomorrow we are marching . . . *(etc.)*

"Console yourself, my dear sweetheart,
Many a flower blooms in May!
Love is not yet over! Over, over . . . !"

Das himmlische Leben
Heavenly life

[Mahler's original orchestral version of this music is a setting for soprano solo in the fourth movement of his Symphony No. 4 in G major, composed in 1892 and 1899–1900, then revised in 1910. The full score carries the footnote: "To be sung with childlike and serene expression; absolutely without parody!"]

We enjoy the heavenly delights,
Therefore do we shun the earthly.
No worldly tumult is heard in heaven!
All live in balmiest peace!
We lead an angelic life!
But we are quite merry at the same time!
We dance and skip, we frisk and sing!
Saint Peter in heaven looks on!
John lets out the little lamb,
The butcher Herod lies in wait for it!
We lead a patient, innocent, patient,
Darling little lamb to its death!
Saint Luke slaughters the ox
Without any hesitation or concern,
The wine costs not a penny in the heavenly cellar,
The angels bake the bread.
Good vegetables of every kind
Grow in the heavenly garden!
Good asparagus, beans and whatever we may desire!
Whole tureens-full are prepared for us!
Good apples, good pears and good grapes!
The gardeners make room for everything!
If you want deer or hare, they come running to you
Along the open road! Should a fast day perchance arrive,
All the fish swim by at once gladly!
There runs Saint Peter already with net and with bait
Into the heavenly fishpond.
Saint Martha must be the cook!
There is truly no music on earth
With which ours can be compared.
Eleven thousand maidens venture to dance!
Saint Ursula herself laughs to see it!
There is truly no music on earth
With which ours can be compared.
Cecilia and her relatives
Are excellent court musicians!
The angel voices enliven the senses,
So that everyone awakes for joy.

Das irdische Leben
Earthly life
[A.F.]

Der Schildwache Nachtlied
The sentinel's nightsong
[A.F.]

Der Tamboursg'sell
The drummer-boy
[J.B.]

Des Antonius von Padua Fischpredigt
Antonius of Padua's fish sermon
[A.F.]

"Es sungen drei Engel einen süssen Gesang"
"Three angels were singing a sweet song"
[A.F.]

[Mahler's original orchestral setting of *Armer Kinder Bettlerlied* (Poor children's begging song) is the fifth movement of his Symphony No. 3 in D minor, composed in 1893–96 and revised in 1906. "Es sungen . . ." begins this poem sung by women's chorus, children's chorus and alto solo.]

Ich ging mit Lust durch einen grünen Wald
I walked with pleasure through a green forest

I walked with pleasure through a green forest;
I heard the songbirds singing.
They sang so young, they sang so old,
The little forest birds in the green forest!
How glad I was to hear them sing!

Now sing, now sing, Lady Nightingale,
Sing this at my sweetheart's house:
"Come soon, come soon, when it's dark,
When there's no one in the street, (then come to me)
I'll let you in!"

The day passed by, night fell,
He came to his sweetheart's house!
He rapped so gently with the knocker:
"Say, are you asleep or awake, darling?
I've been standing here so long!"

The moon looks in through the little window
At his dear, sweet love;
The nightingale sang all night long:
"You sleepy-headed girl, be careful!
What became of your sweetheart?"

Lied des Verfolgten im Turm
Song of the persecuted man in the tower

PRISONER:
Thoughts are free;
Who can guess them?
They whiz by
Like shadows of night.
No person can know them,
No hunter can shoot them.
There the matter rests:
Thoughts are free!

GIRL:
In the summer it's pleasant to be jolly
On high, wild moors.
There one finds green places.
My dearly beloved sweetheart,
I don't want to part from you!

PRISONER:
And if I'm locked up
In dark dungeons,
All of these are merely
Things done in vain;
For my thoughts
Will tear apart the partitions
And walls—
Thoughts are free!

GIRL:
In summer it's pleasant to be jolly
On high, wild hills.
One is always alone there (on high, wild hills),
One hears no yelling of children there!
One can get fresh air there.*

PRISONER:
Then, be it as it may,
And if it should so happen,
Let everything be done quietly;
[And what refreshes me,]**
My wish and desire,
No one can deny me!
There the matter rests:
Thoughts are free!

GIRL:
My darling, you're singing as merrily here
As a little bird in the grass;
I am standing so sadly by the prison door;
I wish I were dead, I wish I were with you;
Ah, must I then lament eternally?

PRISONER:
And because you lament so,
I renounce love!
And if that's daring,
Well, nothing can torment me!
That way, in my heart, I can
Always laugh and joke.
There the matter rests:
Thoughts are free!

---

*For the German "Luft" (air), one reference suggests that "Lust" is probably the original author's intention. The translation would then be: "One can obtain pleasure there."

**omitted by Mahler

Lob des hohen Verstands
In praise of lofty intelligence

Once in a deep valley
The cuckoo and the nightingale
Made a wager:
To sing for the mastery,
Whether they would win by art or by luck:
The winner would carry away the prize.

The cuckoo said: "If it's all right with you,
I've chosen the judge."
And at once he named the donkey.
"For, since he has two big ears,
He can hear all the better,
And discern what's right!"

They soon flew over to the judge.
When the matter was related to him,
He had them sing.
The nightingale sang charmingly!
The donkey said: "You're muddling things up for me!"
    (Heehaw, heehaw!)
I can't get it into my head!"

Then the cuckoo quickly began
His song, passing through the third, the fourth,
    and the fifth on the scale.
The donkey liked it, he just said: "Wait!
I will pronounce my verdict on you.

"You've sung well, nightingale!
But you, cuckoo, you sing a good chorale!
And you keep the measure perfectly!
I say this in accordance with my lofty intelligence,
And even if it cost an entire country,
I proclaim you the winner!" (Cuckoo! Cuckoo! Heehaw!)

Nicht wiedersehen!
No reunion!

"And now farewell, my dearest sweetheart!
Now I must part from you
Until next summer;
Then I'll come back to you!"

And when the young lad came home,
He started to ask about his sweetheart:
"Where is my dearest sweetheart,
Whom I left here?"

"She lies buried in the churchyard,
Today is the third day.
Grieving and weeping
Brought her to her death!"

"Now I will go to the churchyard,
I will look for my sweetheart's grave;
I will call to her constantly
Until she answers me!"

"Oh, you, my dearest sweetheart,
Open your deep grave!
You hear no bell ringing,
You hear no bird whistling,
You see neither sun nor moon!"

Revelge
The dead drummer
[J.B.]

Rheinlegendchen
Little legend of the Rhine

Sometimes I mow grass by the Neckar,*
Sometimes I mow grass by the Rhine;
Sometimes I have a sweetheart,
Sometimes I'm alone!

What's the good of mowing grass
If the sickle won't cut?
What's the good of a sweetheart
If she won't stay with me?

So, if I am to mow grass
By the Neckar, by the Rhine,
Then I'll throw my golden
Little ring into the water!

It will flow with the Neckar
And flow with the Rhine,
And float down
Deep into the sea!

And if it floats, the little ring,
Then a fish will swallow it!
The little fish shall end up
On the king's table!

The king asked
Whose little ring it might be.
Then my sweetheart said:
"The little ring belongs to me!"

My sweetheart leaped
Up and down the hill
And brought back to me
The fine little gold ring!

"You can mow grass by the Neckar,
You can mow grass by the Rhine!
Just throw your little ring
Into the water each time!"

*the river that flows through Heidelberg

Scheiden und Meiden
Parting and staying apart

Three horsemen rode out through the gate!
    Farewell!
Dear sweetheart looked out the window!
    Farewell!
And if we really must part,
Then hand me your little gold ring!
    Farewell! Farewell!
Yes, parting and staying apart hurts!

Even the baby in the cradle is sometimes taken from us!*
    Farewell!
When will I get my darling back?
    Farewell!
And, if it's not tomorrow, I wish it were today!
It surely would give us both great pleasure!
    Farewell! Farewell!
Yes, parting and staying apart hurts!

*This line is abrupt and obscure because Mahler omits a stanza.

Selbstgefühl
Self-awareness

I don't know what's wrong with me!
I'm not sick and I'm not well,
I seem to be wounded but no wound shows.

I don't know what's wrong with me!
I have an appetite but I don't enjoy my food;
I have money but it means nothing to me.

I don't know what's wrong with me!
I have no snuff at all,
And have not a *kreutzer* in my purse.

I don't know what's wrong with me!
I would also like to get married,
But I can't abide children's yelling.

I don't know what's wrong with me!
Just today I asked the doctor,
Who told me to my face:

"I know what's wrong with you:
You're a fool, and no doubt about it!"
Now I know what's wrong with me!

Starke Einbildungskraft
A vivid imagination

THE GIRL:
"You said you would marry me [literally: take me]
As soon as the summer came!
The summer came,
You didn't marry me!
Come, boy, come marry me! All right?
Will you still marry me?"

THE BOY:
"How am I to take you [in marriage]
When I already have you?
Every time I think about you,
Every time I think about you,
I always feel, I feel, I feel
As if I were already with you."

Trost im Unglück
Solace in sorrow
[A.F.]

Um schlimme Kinder artig zu machen
To make naughty children well-behaved

A gentleman came to the country house
On a beautiful steed. (Cuckoo, cuckoo!)
Then the lady peers out of the window
And says: "My husband isn't home,

"And no one's home but my children;
And the maid is in the washhouse."
The gentleman on his steed
Says to the lady in the house: (Cuckoo, cuckoo!)

"Are they good children, are they naughty children?
Ah, dear lady, ah, tell me quickly! (Cuckoo, cuckoo!)
In my saddlebag I have
Many gifts for obedient children," (Cuckoo, cuckoo!)
The lady said: "Very naughty children!
They don't obey their mother quickly."

Then the gentleman says: "In that case, I am riding home,
I don't need any children of that kind!" (Cuckoo, cuckoo!)
And he rode on his steed
Far, far away from the country house! (Cuckoo, cuckoo!)

Urlicht
Primordial light

[Mahler's original orchestral version of this music is a setting for alto solo in the fourth movement of his Symphony No. 2 in C minor ("Resurrection"), composed in 1888–94.]

O little red rose!
Man lies in the greatest need.
Man lies in the greatest suffering.
How much rather would I be in Heaven!
I came upon a broad road.
There came an angel and wanted to block my way.
Ah no! I did not let myself be turned away!
I am of God, and to God I shall return.
Dear God will grant me a small light,
Will light my way to eternal, blissful life.

Verlorne Müh'
Labor lost
[A.F.]

Wer hat dies Liedlein erdacht?
. . . Up there on the hill . . .
[A.F.]

Wo die schönen Trompeten blasen*
Where the beautiful trumpets blow

"Who, then, is outside knocking at the door,
That he can awaken me so gently, so gently?"
"It is your beloved sweetheart,
Get up and let me in to you!
Why should I remain longer here?
I see the dawn rising,
The dawn, two bright stars.
I want to be with my darling!
With my beloved sweetheart!"
The girl got up and let him in,
She also welcomes him.
"Welcome, my beloved boy!
You were standing out there so long!"
She also extends her snow-white hand to him.
In the distance the nightingale sang;
The girl started to weep.
"Oh, don't weep, my darling!
Oh, don't weep, my darling!
In a year you will be mine.
You will surely become mine
As no other girl on earth is!
O my love on this green earth,
I am going off to war on the green heath;
The green heath is so far away!
Where the beautiful trumpets blow:
There is my house of green turf!"

*This seems to have been conflated by Mahler from more than one poem
in the original *Das Knaben Wunderhorn*, or he may have gotten it from
a late, "contaminated" edition.

Zu Strassburg auf der Schanz'
In Strassburg in the entrenchment

In Strassburg in the entrenchment,
That's where my sorrow began!
I heard the alphorn being blown over yonder,
And I had to swim back to my [Swiss] homeland,
And that was against the regulations!

At an hour into the night
They brought me back;
They led me at once to the captain's quarters!
Oh, God, they fished me out of the river!
It's all up with me!

Tomorrow morning at ten
They'll stand me up in front of the regiment;
I'm supposed to ask for pardon there,
But I'll get what I deserve,
I know that already!

All you comrades-in-arms,
Today you will see me for the last time!
The shepherd boy is the only one at fault!
The alphorn cast a spell over me!
That's what I put the blame on!

TEXT TRANSLATIONS
Of *Five Rückert Songs*

John Bernhoff's English translations of poems by Friedrich Rückert
(1788–1866) appear in the music as text underlays and are not reprinted here.
Their titles are as follows.

Blicke mir nicht in die Lieder
Look not, love, on my work unended

Ich atmet' einen linden Duft
I breathed the breath of blossoms red

Ich bin der Welt abhanden gekommen
O garish world, long since thou hast lost me

Liebst du um Schönheit
Lovst thou but beauty

Um Mitternacht
At midnight hour

Des Knaben Wunderhorn and the Rückert Lieder

Ablösung im Sommer

Changing of the guard in summertime

(Text from *Des Knaben Wunderhorn*)

Mit Humor

Ku-kuk hat sich zu To - de ge - fal-len,

To - de ge - fal-len an ei - ner grü - nen Wei - den! Wei - den! Wei - den!

Ku-kuk ist todt! Ku-kuk ist todt! hat sich zu Tod' ge - fal - len!

possierlich

Wer soll uns denn den Sommer lang die Zeit und Weil' ver - trei - ben?

Ku-kuk! Ku-kuk! Wer
soll uns denn den Som-mer lang die Zeit und Weil' ver - trei - ben?
Ei! Das soll thun Frau Nach - ti - gall! Die sitzt auf grü - nem
Zwei - ge! Die klei - ne, fei - ne Nachti - gall, die lie - be, sü - sse Nachti - gall! Sie

*) Von [bis] kann die Gesangsstimme eventuell nach Bedürfniss des Sängers weggelassen werden.

singt und springt, ist all'-zeit froh, wenn an-dre Vö-gel schwei-gen!

Wir war-ten auf Frau Nach-ti-gall, die wohnt im grü-nen

Ha - ge, und wenn der Ku-kuk zu En-de ist, dann fängt sie an zu schla-gen!

Aus! Aus!

Out! Out!

(Text from *Des Knaben Wunderhorn*)

4

he, juch-he, im grü-nen Mai! Ei, du schwarzbraun's Mäg-de-lein, un-s're Lieb' ist

noch nicht aus, die Lieb' ist noch nicht aus, aus! Trink' du ein Gläs-chen Wein

zur Ge-sund-heit dein und mein! Siehst du die-sen Strauss am Hut? Je - tzo heisst's mar-

schi - ren gut! Nimm das Tüch-lein aus der Tasch', dei - ne Thrän-lein mit abwasch'!

Heu - te mar - schie - ren wir, juch - he, juch - he, im grü - nen Mai, mor - gen mar -

schie - ren wir, juch - he, im grü - nen Mai!" „„Ich will in's Klo - ster geh'n,

weil mein Schatz da - von geht! Wo geht's denn hin, mein Schatz? Gehst du fort,

heut' schon fort? Und kommst nim - mer wie - der? Ach! Wie wird's trau - rig sein

hier___ in dem Städt - chen! Wie bald ver - gisst du mein!

Ich!___ ar - mes Mäd - chen!"" „Mor - gen mar - schie - ren wir, juch -

he, juch - he, im grü - nen Mai! Tröst' dich, mein lie - ber Schatz, im Mai blüh'n gar viel

Blü - me - lein! Die Lieb' ist noch nicht aus! Aus! Aus! Aus! Aus!"

Das irdische Leben

Earthly life

(Text from *Des Knaben Wunderhorn*)

English version by Addie Funk

„Mut - ter, ach Mut - ter, es hun - gert mich,
„Mot - her, o Mot - her, so hung - ry I,
gib mir
give me

Brot, sonst ster - be ich!"
bread or I shall die!"

„„War - te nur, war - te nur, mein lie - bes
„„Wait a while, wait a while, my dar - ling

Kind! Mor - gen wol - len wir bak - ken ge - schwind!" "
o, we to - mor - row ba - king will go.""

Und als das Brot ge- bak- ken_ war,
And when the bread was_ ba- ked next day,

lag das
cold the

Kind auf der To - - ten - bahr!_____
child in the cof - - fin lay!_____

Der Schildwache Nachtlied

The sentinel's nightsong

English version by Addie Funk

(Text from *Des Knaben Wunderhorn*)

Zum Waf - fen gar - - - ten!
Have tryst full bit - - - ter!

Voll Hel - le par - - - - ten!
Where hal - berds glit - - - - ter!

Bin ich ge - stellt!
There is my post!

Bin ich ge - stellt!
There is my post!

(verklingend)
(dying away)

Der Tamboursg'scll
The drummer-boy
(Text from *Des Knaben Wunderhorn*)

English version by John Bernhoff

Gu - te Nacht! _____ Gu - te Nacht! _____ Ihr __
Now, good night! _____ *Now, good night!* _____ *Ye* __

Of - fi - zier, Kor - po - ral und Gre - na - dier!
com - rades_ dear, ser - geant, chief and gren - a - dier!

Ich schrei' mit __ hel - ler __
Once more, and __ loud I __

Stimm': von Euch ich __ Ur - laub nimm! _____
call: one last fare well to __ all! _____

Des Antonius von Padua Fischpredigt

Antonius of Padua's fish sermon

(Text from *Des Knaben Wunderhorn*)

English version by Addie Funk

An - to - nius zur Pre - digt die Kir - che find't
An - to - nius for ser - vice the church finds de -

le - dig! Er geht zu den Flüs - sen und pre - digt den Fi - schen! Sie
ser - ted! He goes to the ri - vers to preach to the fi - shes! They

sempre stacc.

30

Kein Pre-digt nie - ma - len
Fish nc'- er like the pre - sent
den
found

Fi - schen so— g'fal - len!
ser - mon so— plea - sant! (mit Humor)
(with humor)

Spitz -
And

go - sche - te Hech - te, die im - mer - zu fech - ten, sind ei - lends her - schwom - men, zu
pike so sharp snou - ted who o - thers have rou - ted in num - bers come spee - ding to the

hö - ren den From - men! Auch je - ne Phan - ta - sten, die im - mer - zu fa - sten: die
Ho - ly Man's rea - ding. The bi - got - ted e - ven, for fas - ting much gi - ven: to

Stock - fisch ich mei - ne, zur Pre - digt er - schei - nen! Kein
cod I'm al - lu - ding, their heads are pro - tru - ding! Cod

Pre - digt nie - ma - len den Stock - fisch so g'fal - len!
ne' - er like the pre - sent found ser - mon so plea - sant! (mit Parodie) (As if in parody.)

Gut
Proud

"Es sungen drei Engel einen süssen Gesang"

"Three angels were singing a sweet song"

(Text from *Des Knaben Wunderhorn*)

Arranged from *Armer Kinder Betterlied*
(Poor children's begging song) in Symphony No. 3

Ich ging mit Lust durch einen grünen Wald

I walked with pleasure through a green forest

(Text from *Des Knaben Wunderhorn*)

45

Etwas langsamer.

Der Tag ver - ging, die Nacht brach an, er kam zu Feins - lieb - chen, Feins-

lieb - chen ge - gan - gen! Er klopft so leis' wohl an den Ring, ei, schläfst du o - der

wachst, mein Kind? Ich hab' so lang' ge - stan - den, ich hab' so lang' ge - standen!

Es schaut der Mond durch's Fen - ster-

Tempo I.

immer Ped.

Lied des Verfolgten im Turm

Song of the persecuted man in the tower

(Text from *Des Knaben Wunderhorn*)

49

Verzagt, schmeichlerisch.

Lob des hohen Verstands

In praise of lofty intelligence

(Text from *Des Knaben Wunderhorn*)

Einst-mals in ei-nem tie-fen Thal Ku - kuk und

Nach - ti-gall thä - ten ein Wett' an - schla — gen: Zu sin-gen um das

Mei-ster-stück, ge-winn' es Kunst, ge-winn' es Glück: Dank soll er da - von tra - gen.

58

ken - nen!" Sie flo-gen vor den Rich-ter bald. Wie dem die Sa-che

ward er-zählt, schuf er, sie soll-ten sin - gen.

Die

Nach-ti - gall sang lieb-lich aus! Der E - sel sprach:„Du

machst mir's kraus! Du machst mir's kraus! I - ja! I - ja! Ich kann's in Kopf nicht brin - gen!"

Der Ku - kuk drauf fing an ge-schwind sein Sang durch Terz und Quart und Quint.

Dem E - sel g'fiels, er sprach nur:"Wart! Wart! Wart! Dein

Ur - theil will ich spre - chen, ja spre - chen. Wohl sun-gen hast du,

Nicht wiedersehen!

No reunion!

(Text from *Des Knaben Wunderhorn*)

junge Knab' heim kam, von sei-ner Lieb-sten fing er an: „Wo

ist mei-ne Herz-al-ler-lieb-ste, die ich ver-las-sen hab'?"

mf *p*

„Auf dem Kirch-hof liegt sie be-gra-ben, heut' ist's der drit-te

pp

ppp Wie fernes Glockenläuten.

℗ed.

sempre pp

Tag! Das Trau-ern und das Wei-nen hat sie zum Tod ge-bracht!" A-

sempre pp *fp*

du, mein al - ler - herz - lieb - ster Schatz, mach' auf dein tie - fes Grab! Du

hörst kein Glöck - lein läu - ten, du hörst kein Vög - lein pfei - fen, du

siehst we - der Son - ne noch Mond! A - de, a - de, mein herz - al - ler - lieb - ster

Schatz, mein herz - al - ler - lieb - ster Schatz! A - de!

Revelge
The dead drummer

(Text from *Des Knaben Wunderhorn*)

English version by John Bernhoff

lie - gen wie ge - mäht.
Death his har - vest reaps.

Er schlägt die Trommel auf und nie - - der, er
He strikes the drum with death-like rat - - tle, each

Glied.
file.

Die___ Trom-mel steht vor-an, die___ Trom-mel steht vor-an, daß
The___ drum-mer heads the train, the___ drum-mer heads the train, that__

sie ihn se - hen kann, tral-la - li, tralla-
she may see her swain, tral-la - lee, tralla-

ley, tral-la - li, tral-la-ley, tralla - le - ra, daß
ly, tral-la - lee, tral-la-ly, tralla - lay - ra, that

sie ihn se - hen kann!
she may see her swain.

Rheinlegendchen

Little legend of the Rhine

(Text from *Des Knaben Wunderhorn*)

Bald gras' ich am Nek-kar, bald gras' ich am Rhein, bald hab' ich ein Schät-zel, bald

bin ich al lein! Was hilft mir das Gra sen, wenn d'Si chel nicht schneid't, was hilft mir ein

Schät zel, wenn's bei mir nicht bleibt!

So soll ich denn gra sen am Nek - kar, am Rhein; so

werf' ich mein gol - de - nes Ring-lein hin - ein! Es

Scheiden und Meiden

Parting and staying apart

(Text from *Des Knaben Wunderhorn*)

Selbstgefühl

Self-awareness

(Text from *Des Knaben Wunderhorn*)

In verdriesslichem Ton.

Ich weiss nicht, wie mir ist! Ich bin nicht krank und nicht ge-
sund, ich bin bles - sirt und hab' kein Wund', ich weiss nicht, wie mir
ist!___ Ich thät' gern es - sen und schmeckt mir nichts; ich hab' ein Geld und gilt mir
nichts, ich hab' ein Geld und gilt mir nichts, ich weiss nicht, wie mir ist! Ich hab' so-

*) Im Nothfalle kann vom Spieler das ganze Stück hindurch die obere Oktave in der linken Hand fortgelassen werden.

heut' den Dok-tor ge-fragt, der hat mir's in's Ge-sicht ge-sagt: „Ich weiss wohl', was dir

ist, was dir ist: Ein Narr bist du ge-

wiss!" „„Nun weiss ich, wie mir ist, nun weiss ich, wie mir ist;"" „ein Narr bist du ge-

wiss!" „„Nun weiss ich, wie mir ist, nun weiss ich, wie mir ist!""

Starke Einbildungskraft

A vivid imagination

(Text from *Des Knaben Wunderhorn*)

Trost im Unglück

Solace in sorrow

(Text from *Des Knaben Wunderhorn*)

English version by Addie Funk

an! Die Zeit ist kom-men! Mein Pferd, das muss ge-sat-telt sein! Ich
then, *'tis time for* *part - ing,* *my* *steed it must be sad-dled now, I've*

hab' mir's vor-ge - nom - men, ge - rit - ten muss es
set my mind on start - ing, *a - rid-ing I must*

sein! Geh' du nur hin!
go. *Do thou but go,*

Ich hab' mein Theil! Ich lieb' dich nur aus Nar - re-thei! Ohn'
I've had my fill, I love thee but from fol - ly still. Can

Um schlimme Kinder artig zu machen

To make naughty children well-behaved

(Text from *Des Knaben Wunderhorn*)

mei-ner Tasch' für folg-sam Kind' da hab' ich manche An - ge-bind;"'ku - ku - kuk, ku-ku - kuk! Die

Oberstimme etwas hervortretend.

Frau, die sagt:„sehr bö - se Kind! Sie fol-gen Muttern nicht geschwind, sind bö - se, sind bö - se!"Die

Frau, die sagt:„sind bö - se Kind! Sie fol - gen, sie fol - gen der Mut-ter nicht geschwind!" Da

*) Zur Erleichterung des Spielers kann in beiden Händen die untere Octave weggelassen werden.

Urlicht

Primordial light

(Text from *Des Knaben Wunderhorn*)

Arranged from the alto solo in
Symphony No. 2 ("Resurrection")

Verlorne Müh'

Labor lost

(Text from *Des Knaben Wunderhorn*)

English version by Addie Funk

Wer hat dies Liedlein erdacht?

...Up there on the hill...

(Text from *Des Knaben Wunderhorn*)

English version by Addie Funk

Mit heiterem Behagen. *With easy gaiety.*

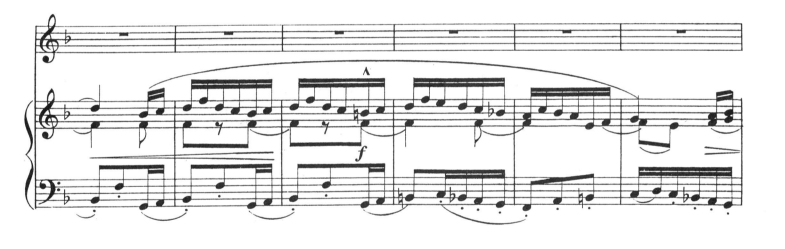

Dort o - ben am Berg in dem ho - - hen Haus! In dem
Up there on the hill in the house so high, house so

Wo die schönen Trompeten blasen

Where the beautiful trumpets blow

(Text from *Des Knaben Wunderhorn*)

lang hast du_ ge - stan - - den! Sie

reicht' ihm auch die_ schnee-wei-sse Hand. Von

fer - ne sang die Nach-ti- - gall, das Mäd-chen fing_ zu wei - - - -

-nen an. Ach

weiß ne nicht, du Lieb - ste mein, ach wei - ne nicht, du Lieb - ste

mein! Auf's Jahr sollst du mein Ei - gen sein.

Mein Ei - gen sollst du wer - den ge - wiss, wie's Kei - ne sonst auf

Er - den ist!_ O Lieb auf grü - - ner Er - - - - -

Zu Strassburg auf der Schanz'

In Strassburg in the entrenchment

(Text from *Des Knaben Wunderhorn*)

Im Volkston (*ohne Sentimentalität, äusserst rythmisch*).

(Wie eine Schalmei.)

Mit starkem Pedalgebrauch.

In gemessenem Marschtempo.

ein wenig zurückhaltend

Strassburg auf der Schanz', da ging mein Trau-ern an!

Das Alp - horn hört' ich

drü - ben wohl an - stim - men, in's Va - ter-land musst' ich hin - ü - ber schwim-men, das

ging ja nicht an, das ging ja nicht an!

*) In allen diesen tiefen Trillern ist mit Hilfe des Pedals der Klang gedämpfter Trommeln nachzuahmen.

124

soll da bit-ten um Par - don, um Par-don! und ich be - komm' doch mei - nen Lohn und ich be -

komm' doch mei - nen Lohn! Das weiss ich schon, das weiss ich schon!

Brü - der all' zu - mal, ihr Brü - der all' zu -

Rückert Lieder

Blicke mir nicht in die Lieder

Look not, love, on my work unended

(Poem by Friedrich Rückert)

English version by John Bernhoff

Blik - ke mir___
Look   not, love,___

___ nicht in die Lie - der!   Mei - ne___   Au - gen___
___ on my work un - end - ed!   Mine___ own___   eyes___ from my

131

Ich atmet' einen linden Duft

I breathed the breath of blossoms red

English version by John Bernhoff

(Poem by Friedrich Rückert)

Ich bin der Welt abhanden gekommen

O garish world, long since thou hast lost me

(Poem by Friedrich Rückert)

English version by John Bernhoff

Ich bin der Welt_____ ab_han_den ge_kom____men,
O gar_ish world,_____ long since thou hast lost____ me,

mit der ich sonst vie_le Zeit ver_dor_ben; sie hat so lan_ge
whose sweet delights my fond heart once cherished, beyond whose ken thy